AF138657

A German Haunting

Herstellung und Verlag: BOD - Books on Demand, Norderstedt

ISBN 9783738615968

Translated from the German by

Oliver Dubiel

"I am not wasting my time with endless efforts at persuasion. Those things cannot be given any credence. You can only know them, or you don't."

Table of Contents

Prologue

Nowadays, haunting does not have a place in our sophisticated society anymore. Simply the openly manifested interest in said topic, or related ones, will be answered with a shake of the head and lack of understanding by surrounding people. Before we damage the reputation for good, let us avert from this matter in order to return to the most up-to-date scientific knowledge. Problem solved! What remains, is an embarrassing memory of an esoteric, crazy idea that we did not believe to be true in the first place. What if, however, one does not believe in haunting, but much rather knows that it actually exists, because he or she has been directly affected by it? The view of the world, acquired over centuries, impends to tilt. Moreover, one is utterly scared of getting up in his or her own house. Who can be addressed concerning this matter and who could possibly lead the way out of this inconceivable situation? Due to the fact that I have been witness of this impossibility

Prologue

for almost thirty years, I was able to accumulate knowledge and experience that I would like to share with the interested, but most importantly, with the readers who are directly affected. I am neither capable of illustrating a solution process nor able to provide a thorough explanation. Nonetheless, I would like to encourage the reader to actively occupy oneself with this subject.

Within the rubric of esotericism, online shops offer a lot of material on haunting, afterlife, and numerous other subjects that can all be classified as supernatural. With that said, why do I need to write another book? I chose to do it for several different reasons. On the one hand, it is human nature to have the desire to tell fellow people about any extraordinary events or experiences. The extraordinary I personally got to experience is extremely encompassing and for that reason, I considered it the proper thing to write the little book you are currently holding in your hands. Even if I cannot necessarily avoid having put the esotericism stamp on my book,

Prologue

I would still like to encourage you to be open-minded and unbiased, because this book has absolutely nothing to do with said topic. I am not interested in selling a certain approach to life, but much rather excited to share words of clarification and resolution. The things we get to read about haunting are usually reports of third parties. Rarely, you will find protocols of individuals directly affected. As a person, who is directly influenced by such phenomena, you develop a different viewpoint than the person who has only heard about the matter from stories. Among other things, I have read numerous books on the topic that "scientifically" deal with parapsychology and discovered interesting perceptions and hypotheses. Again, as a person who knows from own experience that haunting certainly exists I did not have the motivation to deal with the question whether or not this phenomenon really occurs. I simply could not identify with the words on paper or connect my understanding of haunting with that of others. With this book, I hope to offer the reader a better insight into something that

Prologue

anybody could be affected by, although the possibility gets ignored by most people. Or are you only interested in the subject itself and enjoy hearing scary stories? Do not think yourself too safe, because haunting could become a part of your own reality tomorrow!

Xanten, June 2014
B. Creemers

*

Introduction

Because you bought or rented the book at hand, I just assume that you are interested in a phenomenon that the majority of people believe to be nonexistent. When one starts to expose oneself to such a subject matter and openly discusses it, like you and I, he or she normally just gets smiled at since it does not fit in our enlightened view of the world. Enlightened? I would rather call it ignorant! Ignoring processes that have continuously been reported or being told by numerous righteous witnesses for centuries, just because one cannot or is unwilling to comprehend, has little to nothing to do with enlightenment and sophistication. Considered from a scientific point of view, it is obviously difficult to prove something that somewhat sticks to a known rule. But do we not already live with or among things whose mechanism of action we cannot necessarily explain? Today, hardly anybody questions the efficacy of acupuncture, even though the practice bases its methods on a totally different picture of the human body than widely accepted science. Meanwhile, insurance policies even include certain diagnosis and treatment according to a traditional Chinese medicine, although it would have to be considered humbug from a modern scientific perspective. The fewest have a problem with it and alternative treatment methods, which seem to detract from every scientific foundation, tend to be offered in many places and are briskly practiced. We are receptive and approachable with respect to these methods, for a good reason: they have demonstrated a positive effect on our overall well-being and have therefore earned eligibility in our health care system. In my opinion, the question whether or not haunting is real, can be treated similarly. It is not clear which powers operate and why they do, but they have a severe effect on the person affected. This effect, however, different from alternative treatment methods, is generally not the cause for an increase in the well-being, but much rather a negative influence. This harm can range from fear and mental disturbance of the "victims" to substantial property damage. Presumably, such conditions are partly responsible for the general denial and rejection. More often than not, religious people are better off concerning this matter, as the different religions offer compelling evidence for such anomalies. Angels, demons, ghosts, or even the direct involvement of the respective divine figure, for the purpose of punishment for example, are offered as sufficient explanation. Catholics can make use of certain offers of assistance in the form of pastoral ministry. Particularly, the practice of exorcising demons falls within the scope of pastoral ministry within the Catholic Church.

Haunting, poltergeists, affliction, supernatural phenomena, paranormal experience, and recurrent spontaneous psycho kinesis (RSPK) are just a few names for a phenomenon complex that is too indescribable and comprising in order to be able to find a summarizing, generally applicable term soon.

Introduction

Principally, I utilize the term haunting, because it gives no evidence about person's belief and leaves space for different interpretations. Nevertheless, everybody understands what is being talked about. In order to deal with haunting, one has to be willing to accept something as existent that should normally not be there. Of course, one needs to strictly examine and objectively investigate in all possible directions. The possibility of fraud or the natural, but unknown, phenomenon to the observer is certainly given.

Outsiders will quite often pretend to have this "natural" explanation for an answer in order to avoid burdening themselves with this unimaginable reality. According to my opinion, this specific behavior is completely normal and understandable. As a person affected, one has to be clear on this topic, before one attempts to entrust oneself to third parties. Those who come in for these indecent and inexplicable activities have one thing in common: fear. Initially, victims try to find an easy explanation by blaming these irregularities on their own scattiness, or special coincidences and accidents. If the intensity of the haunting increases, however, the view of the world seems to be endangered and one feels pressured to validate or revise some dogmas or abandon them altogether. Promising assistance in contention with this topic can normally not be expected, not even from individuals that are usually being consulted with certain matters of concern. Therefore, many do not have any options but to endure and withstand and to try to avoid losing one's mind, because open discussion generally only leads to further damage. One accepts to be exposed to ridicule or find journalists who have little to no interest in an objective report, compared to a wild story which ends with debunking a fraud, for example. When the haunting is over, one has to start to forget and suppress. Similar to an experience with a severe illness, one chooses not to talk about it and would be happy to rather shelve it entirely. Nevertheless, there are certain cases where

Introduction

normal conditions cannot be reestablished, even after a number of weeks or months. The report about such a case can be found in this book. There is no need for persuasion, because only people who have actually made a haunting experience know that this phenomenon exists. And among other things, this is one reason why I wrote this book at hand for this specific category of persons. A German haunting. Finding help tends to be an almost impossible task to do and for that reason, it is so important for victims to exchange their information and discuss their own problems with fellow sufferers.

*

Haunting during my childhood

I am thirty-four years old, happily married and the proud father of three healthy children. Job wise, I am a content paramedic and for the past twelve years, I have earned my money providing rescue service for the German Red Cross. Up until the age of fourteen, I spent most of my childhood in Duisburg, an industrial city in the Ruhr region of Western Germany, split into forty-six different districts and a population of approximately 490.0000. I was living there with my parents and my sister in rather calm area, characterized by streets of houses with four-story row houses. In one of those houses, on the Moltke Street, we were sharing roughly one hundred square meters on the bottom floor. The apartment had very high ceilings and was equipped with a kitchen, bathroom with a bathtub, living room, master bedroom, winter garden, and a children's room that I had to share with my sister. The walls were painted nut-brown which was probably considered modern and fashionable during the 80s. My father, a man with an exceptionally acute sense and an inclination for jazz and botany, worked an upper position in a steel factory. My mother, a warmhearted person and a mom in and out, drove to the weekly market to sell herbal goodies. My sister, three years younger than me, and I did not go short in any way. Neither did we have too little money nor did our parents miss any opportunity to show their compassion for us. We were on vacation on a regular basis, owned a mid-class estate car, enjoyed excursions on the weekend, and did not go to church, although all family members had been baptized and received the communion. Overall, we could be described as the typical family living in Duisburg during the 80s. Myself, I was a very calm and introversive boy. In kindergarten, the nursery nurses were somewhat troubled to animate me for age-appropriate activities, because I had no interest in finger games and children's dances. When I was allowed, I would draw or occupy myself with other things that did not require making a fool out of me, which is exactly how I perceived most of these activities with regard to an adult's expectation for a child that age. This congruency in between expectations and my own willingness to fulfill these continued from elementary school all the way through high school. My sister was the exact opposite of me. She was an adapted and accommodated child who liked to satisfy everybody's requirements. Both of us got along very well and we rarely got into an argument with each other. That was the basis for a jaunty childhood as I had everything needed in order to grow up healthy. Despite this fact, I did not write the book at hand in order to tell you about my fabulous and inconspicuous youth. In reality, I would like to use this chapter to tell you about that one night I experienced tremendous fear which even took hold of me throughout the day. This specific fear dominated most of my youth and made it hardly bearable at times. I was only able to escape this fear if I was in company or in bright and vivid places. Of course, there are

Haunting during my childhood

many people who suffer from irrational fear or panic attacks who are consequently trying to find psychiatric or psychological treatment, because it is a serious illness. My fear, however, was not an irrational one. There was a good reason for it. It was haunting. If those haunting appearances would have stopped at some point during my youth, I would probably assume that I was suffering from a psychotic episode at that point in time. Unfortunately, even today, that is not the case. The impressions of my past are as present as ever and new ones are being added regularly. In retrospect, there has not been a longer period in my life during which I was not plagued by my own personal "poltergeist." It took a while for me to actively identify myself with this subject matter, as the intensity and tenacity of the phenomena pressured me to do so. Up to that point, I was rather passive and tried to endure or ignore the haunting, while making the experience that this behavior only amplified the sensation. Following this paragraph, I am describing the incidents during my childhood and youth as best as I

Haunting during my childhood

can remember them.

The children's room that I was sharing with my sister was the main site of all the appearances that I can recall. It was about twenty square meters in size and located opposite of the kitchen, separated only by the hallway. It was, different from all the other rooms, painted in white. My bed was placed right next to the window, which was overlooking the street, and my sister's bed next to the door leading into the hallway. The room was inlaid with grey carpet and only consisted of two desks, two dressers, and one shelf. The lighting was coming from a balloon lamp on the roof, desk lamps, and two lamps, in the form of big yellow plugs, installed on the walls of the beds. Overall a neat children's room, as I would have constructed it similarly for my children today, if they were to share a room. As pretty as the room really was, it did not change the unlovely experiences I made in it. One night, when I was about eight years old, I was laying in my bed trying to fall asleep. For some reason, I was not able to though. Suddenly, I realized how I was being pulled upward by a gentle, but nonetheless strong, power. My back lost contact with the mattress and I was floating above it. Completely taken off guard by this situation, I was so scared that I could not even call for help, although I wanted to. I was wide awake and noticed how I got lifted higher and higher off my bed. At a certain height, about thirty centimeters off the mattress, I started to float sideways at unvarying height, legs first, to the center of the room, where I was put down on my back again. Unable to react, I noticed that the room's roof had changed its structure. It did not look like an integral part of the room anymore. Much rather, it resembled a heavy overcast right before a thunderstorm - dark and threatening, moving, cloudy-like structures. I was laying there, not capable of making any sound let alone move around which made the whole situation extremely uncomfortable and horrible. It was silent around me. The atmosphere was forbidding and I was horrified. All of the sudden, I could make out two voices from the silence. They seemed to be coming from the roof. Clearly and concisely I could hear: "Shall we?" and the other one replied: "Yes." Thereupon, I could hear a loud and rhythmic noise. For a few minutes I was laying there, listening to the noise which sounded like the heartbeat of a human being, heard through a stethoscope; though a bit more high pitched. With all my might, I tried to call for help, which I eventually succeeded with, in the end. The call for help was rather timid, but loud enough to alarm my mother who came running into my room. She found my laying on the ground, flat on my back, just the way I was put down. What happened afterwards detracts from my memory. Later, during my teenage years, I talked to my mother about this specific incident, because it had certainly left deep scars. She had perceived the situation as "utterly strange and sinisterly" and admitted to have felt the threatening atmosphere in my room. As a matter of fact, up to this day, she remembers how she picked me up from the floor and put me back in my bed. A similar incident, at a later point in time, had a milder outcome as I was able to avoid the floating by holding on to my bed. The strange power let go off me and I felt the weight of my body drop back into the mattress. Cases of children who report extraordinary experiences during the phases of falling asleep or waking up are sufficiently known. However, I do not consider the described event such a phenomenon, because I can remember too much detail information about that day. I was wide awake, fully conscious, and my physical body was, in fact, moved, which excludes an *out of body experience*. Up to this day, I am having trouble recognizing a further meaning or message from this experience and the statements of the two voices especially. I did not experience any more levitations of this kind though.

The white woman is a constantly resurfacing appearance in literature. For ages and across different cultures, she has been described as a foreboding phantom eager to convey a message or warn the person she meets face to face. She embodies the classical "ghost" – sometimes shadowy or semitransparent, and sometimes a lifelike, lean woman in a white dress. She appears at typical locations like castles and fortresses, but also in a more civilized environment. The Irish call her "Banshee" – ghost woman. I was haunted by an appearance that resembled that of the white woman one night. I was lying in my bed could not fall asleep. At that point, I was probably about twelve years old. I was lying on my side, facing the wall, and suddenly had a hunch that somebody was standing next to my bed (Most people know the feeling of "being watched;" an inexplicable feeling that is generally accepted as natural and occurring, however.). Subsequently, I turned around and saw a woman in a white dress, with a veil, and a baroque-like collar standing next to my bed. She had lowered her head as if she was sad and disappeared only a few seconds after I had turned around. The figure faded, just like the light of a lamp when you turn it off. The scenery was very short in time, but it was one of those encounters you will not forget, because they have a further meaning. At least that is what it felt like. I could never figure out the reason for this strange visit in the evening, however. I cannot recall any fatalities or anything especially remarkable in my direct surroundings. There were multiple events that scared me. In fact, there were doors opening and closing by themselves in front of my eyes or I perceived strange, bodiless voices in close vicinity. From time to time, things were even randomly thrown at me – one time, it was a brick that came flying out of the bushes. Fortunately, I was never hit by one of them. For all those years, I was also accompanied by creatures that I personally named *Ürgies*. Ürgies happened to appear in different forms. There were small Ürgies that were watching me from corners of rooms and big Ürgies that were just lying around and seemed to be somewhat of an alpha leader. It was the big Ürgies that were predominantly appearing in my nightmares. I could see the small Ürgies while I was awake, how they were hanging from the room's roof, watching me. I could only see them when I was by myself, however. I find it difficult to describe the looks of these observers as they did not have any clear contours and were only hazily visible. They had a quadratic form and at their end, which seemed to be the head, pointy ears. To me, they looked threatening and enigmatic. I talked to them, but never received a direct answer in the form of a language. Whenever I addressed them, they responded by making loud *Mimikri* noises. Oftentimes, it was the noise of rattling dishes or simply a loud hubbub of voices. These noises were unnaturally loud and threatening. When I tried to ignore them, they became angry and scared me by wildly pushing the balloon lamp in the children's room on a swing, for example. At first, I could feel their presence when there was a threatening atmosphere spreading in the room. Immediately, I experienced overbearing fear and felt the urge to run away. Sometimes I did, when I was physically able to and could not bear it any longer. In that case, I left the room and looked for the companionship of my parents. An escape was not always possible, because these Ürgies were capable of keeping the door shut. Eventually, I stopped seeing the Ürgies on a regular basis and they had less and less influence on my life, until they disappeared completely. Nevertheless, when I started writing this book, I saw another one of these Ürgies, hanging from the corner of the roof, after a long time. I had the impression as if he was already watching me for a few minutes before I actually spotted him. He disappeared only a few seconds after I had discovered him. Maybe it was only delusion, but probably it was not, because I am extremely critical with the evaluation of my perception, especially in regard to this topic – I saw this Ürgie! Fully conscious, I was able to make out this thirty-five centimeter tall, shadowy creature hanging from the roof.

*

Haunting during my childhood

Depiction of the "White Woman," as she is being described by witnesses for centuries. Those apparitions are often considered to be a portent. In many cases the white woman has been seen shortly before someone has died. Other names for the White Woman are La dame blanche, Weisse Frau, White Goddess, White Lady, Witten Wieven and Moura Encatada.

Haunting during my childhood

Another picture of a female ghost.

Haunting during my childhood

Escalier du Château de Gy.

A perfect place for a haunting? Most hauntings do not occur on graveyards or old castles but amongst the living.

Later years

After we had moved away from Duisburg in 1994, the haunting ran a milder course. Every so often, I experienced particular phenomena, but the intensity had reduced noticeably. What did not decline was my fear of being alone. It was as present as ever, the way I knew it from my early childhood. When I came to rest in the evenings, it was only a matter of time until I felt something around me, watching me and causing this anxiety in me. Occasional throwing of smaller objects and explosions of light bulbs or lighters reminded me of the fact that I was not dealing with pure imagination. Back then, I already suspected that the cause for my haunting appearances was not be found in my direct surroundings, but was rather a problem with myself. Therefore, I undertook the first cautious attempts and tested, for example, if I was able to identify a single card out of a multitude of cards turned upside down by simply concentrating on them. With

Later years

bewildering reliability, I succeeded over and over again, which only confirmed my assumption that haunting had something to do with me. Consistently reappearing anticipations that proved to be well-founded only solidified my suspicion. However, I was intimated by this perception with the result that I stopped pursuing it soon. In the following years, I attached this topic little to no value at all. Not until I turned twenty-two years old, and the phenomena increased in intensity and frequency, I reconsidered the topic. At this point, I was already living with the woman that I call my wife today and my oldest daughter, in a one hundred square meter apartment in the historic part of Xanten. It was our first own apartment and it was located on the first and only floor of an approximately one hundred and fifty year old row house on the Klever street. Here, I frequently noticed the bursting of light bulbs. They literally exploded and splintered into numerous, little shards. Things kept disappearing and reappeared at a later time and a different place. Our daughter had a puppet that alternated between crying and laughing when you put its hands together or just touched both hands at the same time. On the palm of its hands, the puppet had electric wires. When we were at the point of leaving the apartment, said puppet never failed to start crying. It always happened with absolute certainty. Only after we removed the batteries, this behavior discontinued. Other than that, it functioned reliably and without any other disorders. One night, among other things, we remarked that different spoons, forks and pliers in our silverware tray were severely bent, without having a reasonable explanation for it. Time and time again, we sensed steps and knocking during the night. Altogether, the incidents were more harmless, but impossible to ignore. At that point, we rarely talked about them as I did not want to create a connection to the haunting experiences of my childhood. Still, my wife and I were scared.

Two years after, we moved to a much brighter and better equipped apartment. Bursting light bulbs, bent silverware, steps during the night,

Later years

and other phenomena were not uncommon in the new place either. With regard to their intensity and frequency, they were rather weak, but nonetheless unmistakable. It did not become genuinely impressive and overwhelming until we had moved the next time. Because we were expecting further offspring and the apartment offered too little space, we moved to a house within the same city. Shortly after moving in, we already experienced fierce and vigorous appearances that were reason enough for me to actively face up to them. Based on a recommendation of the Institute for Border Areas in Psychology and Mental Hygiene based on Freiburg, I started writing a "haunting diary." I kept said diary predominantly starting from October 2011 until December 2012. Unfortunately, it is way too comprehensive to be able to print it within the frame of this book. On the following pages, I am reciting excerpts of the diary.

*

The Haunting Diary

10.10.2011

Today, I heard pebble stones repeatedly getting thrown against the glass of the windows on the first floor. In front of the house there is an open field and it is impossible to throw pebble stones against the house unseen. Our daughter also noticed the stone-throwing. We supposed she was just playing a prank.

21.10.2011 at around 13:00

My wife and I were sitting in the workroom, on the first floor, and were discussing different issues. The kids were in school and kindergarten, respectively. Suddenly, we could hear loud rattling from downstairs. In the kitchen, we found parts of the kitchen cladding lying in the middle of the room. At the time of the noise, no one was present in the kitchen. The wooden kitchen cladding was not damaged and easily put back in place without any problems.

23.10.2011

We were lying in bed on the first floor, watching TV, late at night. Suddenly, we heard quick, stomping steps in the hallway as if a kid was running on socks. Those steps were moving around unnaturally loud in the hallway upstairs. The kids were already asleep.

01.11.2011 between 06:30 and 07:30

After I had left the house to go to work my wife decided to go back to bed. All the kids were still asleep. When she woke up shortly after, she found a massage cross on top of her chest. This specific cross, made out of tulipwood, was originally lying in the cabinet in the master bedroom. She fell asleep on her back and woke up the exact same way. The door of the cabinet was still locked.

05.11.2011

In the evening, we were sitting on the sofa in

the living room. The kids were sitting on the two armchairs watching TV. My oldest son had spread out a few books on top of the dining room table. My wife drew my attention to one of those books which started to move by itself all of the sudden. Slowly but surely, it was fitfully sliding toward the edge of the table. After roughly a minute, it had reached its destination and fell to the ground. The kids did not witness anything, because they were caught up in a show on TV.

06.11.2011

In the hallway downstairs it smelled like incense or similar incense materials all of the sudden today. We noticed the smell before noon. The smell was spatially limited and only perceivable on roughly two and a half meters of the hallway. At the same time, numerous windows downstairs started to steam within only a few seconds. It was relatively cold outside. The smell and the steam on the windows disappeared after about ten minutes. For about two weeks now, we have heard small stones being thrown against the windows again.

21.11.2011

For a few days, we have repeatedly heard different family members call from down- and upstairs in the evening. Usually, a voice, that sounds just like my own, calls for my wife. Even the voices of the kids are imitated and are calling "Mommy!" or "Daddy!". The dog behaves conspicuously. Oftentimes, he abruptly stares at the corner of the room's roof and shows strong anxiety by drawing in his tail and whimpering. He is too scared to walk by this specific spot of the room.

22.11.2011

Today, my wife was standing in the dining room with her back facing the buffet when a porcelain dish (about 10 centimeters in diameter) fell to the ground and broke into two pieces. Nobody had the chance to catch it. The breaking point was very central and straight.

24.11.2011 around 23:00

Yesterday evening I was lying in bed with my son Louis, because he had trouble falling asleep. When I had fallen asleep myself, I was awoken by the barking of our Great Dane Hannelore and several calls. My husband was loudly yelling: "No, Hanni, no!" In horror, I realized that I was incapable of moving and speaking. It felt like somebody was strongly pushing my ankles and chest onto the mattress. When I finally managed to call for help, my husband came into the children's room and turned on the light. Immediately, the pressure on me wore off and I was able to move and speak without a problem, as usual. My son was sound asleep and did not seem to have noticed anything. My husband and I walked into our bedroom and I told him that I had heard him yelling. He assured me that neither he nor the dog made any sound at all.

27.11.2011

My wife and I were sitting upstairs. The kids were on the bottom floor. Suddenly, we could hear loud rumbling from downstairs as if a train was driving through our house. The kids were screaming. We stormed downstairs. Everything was calm. Sophia explained that the whole kitchen had been shaking. Apparently, the washing machine almost fell over. I examined everything, but I could not find any suspicious features. Merely the pots on top of the stove had changed positions and parts of the kitchen cladding were lying on the floor.

My wife and I went back upstairs. When we got to the bedroom, we felt a cold airflow. The whole room was certainly much colder than it was before. Anke notified me about the two anatomy posters in the hallway, on the wall, that were hanging on the wall upside down. One of them was incessantly swinging. Even in the hallway, the temperature had noticeably dropped.

<u>13.12.2011</u>

In the corners of the ceilings of the bedroom and living room we could make out lightening for the past two days — very bright lightning bolts that successfully lit up the room, even during daylight. In the past, we were able to regularly watch these lightning bolts. Today, we noticed another extraordinarily large amount of them.

27.12.2011

In the past few weeks, I noticed the usual appearances. Things disappeared and reappeared, lightning bolts under the ceilings, rumbling and mysterious steps during the night, vibration of our bed, and other phenomena. Today, it was raining from the ceiling of our living room while the ceiling itself did not get wet. Very small drops of water rained down on me for about five minutes. My arms were wet afterwards. The sofa I was sitting on and other circumjacent objects were also dampened.

12.01.2012

For several days already, objects kept disappearing; especially those that you need on a daily basis. They reappear in the most random and uncommon places. That is how my glasses disappeared, for example. I certainly placed them on the buffet previously, only to find them on the window sill outside, on accident. Something similar happened with various cigarette packs and other objects. Over and over, things fell over without seeing an apparitional trigger for it. This evening, at around 22:05, a screwdriver fell on my foot while I was leaving the bathroom on the first floor. The screwdriver happened to appear out of nowhere, directly above my head, and fell down in a straight line, viciously aiming for my foot. I did not get injured, but it hurt nonetheless. I called for my wife and explained the incident to her. After that, I picked up the screwdriver and noticed a recognizable heating of the upper part.

<u>20.01.2012</u>

The attic can only be reached through a flap in the ceiling of the hallway upstairs. When opening said flap, a hinged ladder unfolds.

The Haunting Diary

Today, at around 17:50, Anke opened the flap to access the attic. Somebody must have put boxes on top of the flap and the folded ladder as they plunged after opening the flap, and spilled all over the floor. Putting boxes on top of the folded ladder and closing the flap afterwards is sheer impossible. There is no other access to the attic. The boxes have placed themselves on the flap so that they had to fall down when my wife opened the flap; similar to a trap.

05.02.2012

While I was eating in the staff restaurant of the hospital today, I recognized how the teeth of my fork bent after a few minutes. It caught my attention, because they bent drastically enough for me to notice when I moved the fork toward my mouth. Initially, the fork was in a perfect condition. The fork's teeth kept bending, even after I had already noticed the phenomenon. In the end, it turned out to be extremely uncomfortable having to eat with this specific fork, because the bent teeth were simply annoying. Time and time again, spoons and forks started to bend after I had picked them up. Concerning the forks, it was only the teeth. The spoons bend at their weakest and thinnest point.

07.02.2012

A Buddha bust, which is standing on a shelf, was turned so that it was now facing the shelf's wall. Nobody had watched or caught said instance. However, it can be precluded that a family had turned the bust, because it is out of reach for the kids and neither I nor my wife had turned the bust. I perceived the sight of the "wall-facing Buddha" as a kind of desecration.

20.02.2012

For a few days, we have attempted to record certain phenomena with the help of two infrared cameras. They are running in an infinite loop at night. Up to this point, we could only film the cap of a cardboard box that closed itself at night along with a handful of other light appearances. Constantly, water faucets started to turn on randomly. The water is streaming out relatively slowly. Today, this scenario resulted in considerable water damage due to the fact that the sink in the bathroom upstairs was clogged. The water faucet opened in our absence and the sink overflowed. The fire truck toy drove itself out of its garage and did not stop until it reached the edge of the carpet.

03.03.2012

The light on the first floor does not function properly anymore. We put in LED lights, hoping they would last a little bit longer. The lamp, a string of three different lights, flares or does not work at all. When you ask for light, however, the lamp turns on and illuminates the room as long as you are close by.

06.03.2012

I can hear a loud clapping of hands in the hallway. It was calm in the apartment and nobody was even moving around in the hallway. Nevertheless, the sound could be accurately identified as clapping of hands.

14.03.2012

This past night, the bed had vibrated so violently that my wife woke up from it. I had not fallen asleep yet and it started vibrating thirty seconds before my wife woke up. Altogether, for a whole minute, it was vibrating so bad that it was literally shaking.

24.04.2012

Because of the frequency of the phenomena and the fact that we have lost interest in keeping up with the diary, we have not made any entries in the last few weeks. Here is to sum up the definite "irregularities" of the past few weeks:

The heavy oven in the kitchen has been rumbling around loudly and fitfully. The oven was turned off and the rumbling lasted several seconds.

The Haunting Diary

Several key chains kept disappearing all of the sudden and were rediscovered hanging in the key box. Nobody in the family has placed those keys there and the box is usually never in use anyway.

My cell phone disappears without a trace. Within the next instant, it reappears in the middle of the sofa. I checked the sofa beforehand. When I picked up the phone, it was very warm, almost hot. Even minutes after that spectacle, it still had a surprisingly high temperature.

I found razorblades on the edge of the bathtub; the kind of razorblades that nobody uses in our household. I found the same kind of blades on my desk all of the sudden. They are noticeably warmed up. All of them are coated with a kind of film of oil.

When I am at work, my wife receives calls from the office or vice versa, without anybody saying a word. It seems as if my wife's cell phone independently dials the number and the phone at work independently calls my wife. Often, it is several times in row.

My wife put the vacuum cleaner in the hallway upstairs. When she wanted to start vacuuming, it disappeared. After a long search, she finally found it in the hallway downstairs. It was standing on top of a shelf. In the dining room, candles lit by themselves.

Still, light bulbs fell out of their sockets or burst altogether.
Twice, I am pelted with a book. One of those books was placed on a shelf, the other one on a cabinet. Both of them hit me in the chest, only to fall to the ground thereafter.

A glass flies out of an open cabinet curving toward the heater, where it bursts.

We decided to continue keeping up with the diary, because, as direct witnesses, we thought it was important to document the strange phenomena.

The Haunting Diary

<u>13.05.2012</u>

Faucets turned on automatically. Miscellaneous, smaller   incidents.
This morning, the big, round carpet in the living room was turned upside tow, now showing the bottom side.

<u>16.05.2012</u>

At night, my wife observed how my blanket was pulled away toward my feet. The blanket was grabbed at one of its corners and pulled slowly. When I was uncovered up to my knees, the blanket was let go again. I personally did not notice anything. My wife was awake at that point, because she had woken up from knocking noises coming from the hallway.

<u>22.05.2012</u>

I was driving to work on the interstate road this morning. Traffic was moving quickly when some kind of movie started acting out in front of my "inner eye" all of the sudden. I saw debris of a car flying past me. Grey plastic pieces of a bumper bar as well as laminated glass splinters. It looked like some sort of explosion four or five cars further up. This "movie" lasted about three or four seconds. Roughly a minute later, that is exactly what happened. A vehicle, driving about 4 cars in front of me, drove straight into oncoming traffic and all I could see were splinters and plastic pieces flying through the air.

02.06.2012

Shortly after the alarm went off today, we heard loud rumbling and banging from the kitchen. My wife and I started looking and noticed that the dining table lamp had fallen off the ceiling. It was barely hanging on the electrical wire and swinging from left to right. The glass, surrounding the light bulbs, was destroyed. I checked the dowels the lamp was hanging on. They were still strongly grounded in the ceiling. The screws, that were holding lamp, were also still intact. I screwed the screws back into the dowels and they were fixed in place. It seems as if the screws had unscrewed themselves.

08.06.2012

Today, a painting kept falling off the wall which has been hanging there for months. Whenever we put it back up on the wall, it only took a few minutes for it to fall down again. We always found it facing us with the front side. One time, it was lying on an armchair that is about two meters away from the spot where the painting is normally hanging on the wall. The frame of the painting is firmly resting under a strongly driven in screw. It represents a Buddha figure with bamboo.

21.06.2012

The computer screen has turned about thirty degrees clockwise. At that time, I was watching TV and could only see the movement out of the corner of my eye. During the evening, I heard knocking noises that I was able to localize in different spots of a wall in the living room. The knocking sounded like somebody was knocking their ankles strongly against the wall.

The Haunting Diary

<u>10.07.2012</u>

Lately, it has been lightening more frequently in the corners of various rooms' ceilings again. The lightning bolts consist of white light that does not fully illuminate the room, almost as if it was stopping at a certain distance from its origin.

<u>17.07.2012</u>

My hands get cut up. Over a span of about three days, cuts start to appear on my hands. They are red and sometimes even bleed a little bit. More and more cuts add to the existing ones and they burn. The back of my hands are affected most particularly.

<u>19.07.2012</u>

The cuts on my hands have completely disappeared overnight. Today, I felt vigorous vibrations of the bed frame when I had laid down for an afternoon nap.

The Haunting Diary

This morning, all pictures in the living room were hanging on the wall crooked. The clock on the kitchen wall had turned itself one-hundred-eighty degrees so that the six was now on top. Nobody had seen the twisting and turning of the pictures and the clock, as those movements must have happened throughout the night.

24.07.2012

Today, my wife was pelted with a Tupperware container. It flew out of an opened cabinet base, all the way through the kitchen, and hit her in the pelvis. The flight path must have been from the bottom upwards. At that time, she was in the apartment by herself and did not personally witness the flight of the container.

27.07.2012

For several days now, we keep finding our toothbrushes and other objects out of the bathroom in the cat litter box. Every time, it is objects that are meant for the body's hygiene and that need to be thrown away after they had been resting in the cat litter box for a while. The cat litter box itself is also in the bathroom, but it is impossible for the cat to move those objects itself.

<u>11.08.2012</u>

In the last few days, we have tried to avoid said topic, because I can hardly sleep at night anymore.

<u>05.12.2012</u>

I have been looking for my favorite jacket for almost a year. It disappeared out of nowhere and over the course of the next few months we had inspected every single corner in the apartment. This evening, it was hanging on the wardrobe as if it had always been there. It was a heavy, oversized anorak.

<u>21.12.2012</u>

My wife was pelted with baubles from the Christmas tree. She was standing about two meters away from the tree. The baubles swerved our son, who was standing in between the tree and my wife, and hit my wife straight into the stomach and chest.

The records end in December 2012. Between May and December 2012, we have only made occasional entries, because I was mainly focused on researching the topic haunting. Therefore, the diary faded into the background. The reason for the diary was to record the incidents in order to have the chance to detect a pattern from the overall picture. Unfortunately, we did not find the reason for all the haunting appearances. Also, we could not discover any hidden messages within the phenomena. We confined ourselves to using an infrared camera that was filming nearly every night and whose material I always examined the following day. We specifically filmed all the locations that were predominantly known for their phenomena. I did not expect much as I knew from pertinent literature that haunting appearances elude from direct surveillance. They take place in the corner of an eye or at the time when nobody is watching. Oftentimes, one can only see the outcomes. Out of many hours of material, I was only able to filter out a handful of sequences which showed things that could not be explained easily. Three times, the camera had recorded light phenomena and one time I could see how a closed door opened a tiny crack. However, I usually noticed noises in the recordings. Strange hubbub and loud rumbling were among the most frequent ones.

At this time, I repeatedly approached the German Institute for Border Areas in Psychology and Psycho hygiene (IGPP) in Freiburg hoping to find some help with my problems. I was advised to search for significance in all the individual incidents. I was told to try and interpret them in order to recognize a specific statement. According to the *animistic theory*, haunting is a shift of unconscious problems of a human being to his surroundings. In that case, phenomena actually do take place and are triggered unconsciously by the so-called "focus person." If the person realizes the problem at hand the haunting should stop, because its meaning would be to call attention to the hidden problem. However, up to this day, I have yet to find a hidden message or clue. I have come to realize a totally different explanation for my experiences, but I will mention that at a later point. The experiences explained in this chapter are only a small extract out of a plethora of outlandishness that I have lived through in the past few years. Even today, my wife and I notice something similar almost daily. Still, the glass of the light bulbs came loose from its socket and fell to the ground, for example. Things disappear and reappear; a guise is continuously seen by my wife and children. It is usually walking back and forth in the hallway. Silverware bends and steps are being heard when nobody could be the cause. The light turns on and off by itself and water faucets do the exact same thing. One time, I was able to witness how a metal cross bent in front of my own eyes. I had ordered the cross and when the package arrived, I opened it, and found it in an impeccable condition. It was standing on a curved platform and a Jesus figure was affixed. After I had put it in the cabinet and watched it for a while I saw how it bent forward, making little Jesus face the ground. Immediately, I took it back out of the cabinet and straightened it out, which required lots of power.

The Haunting Diary

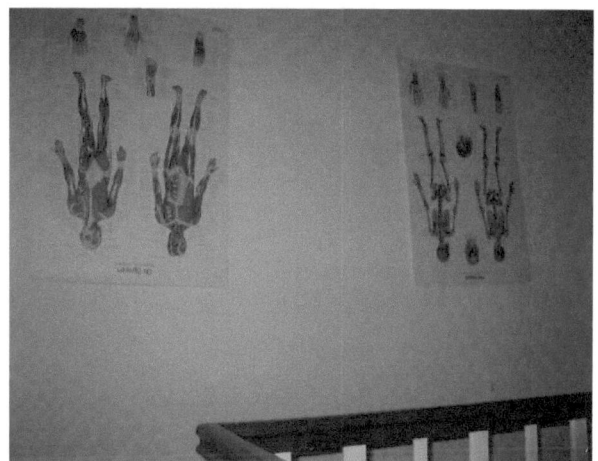

Picture 1, 27.11.2011

Picture 2

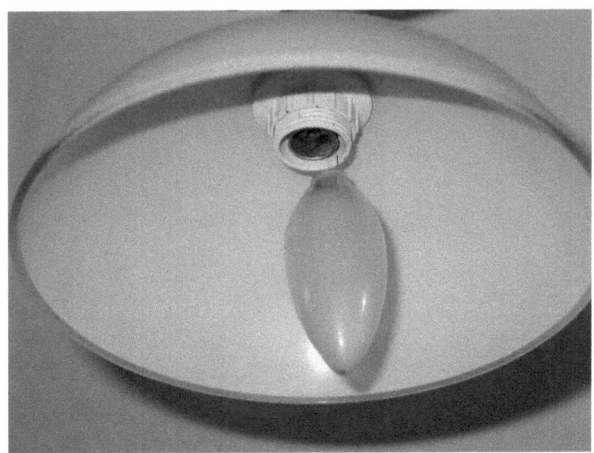

Picture 3

Picture 4

Picture number 1 shows an original photo of the anatomy posters wich turned upside down.

Picture number 2 shows an original photo of the kitchen after the doors opened by itself.

Picture number 3 and number 4 show original photos of defect bulbs. Most bulbs come apart like those on the photo.

This knife broke while it was toweled with no force.

The Haunting Diary

Frequently, our bed vibrates so violently that it starts moving – similar to an electric razor that you put down while it is switched on.

In preparation for a phone conversation with the IGPP, I drew up a table with the current phenomena. Such a table assists in keeping a better overview and projects one's thoughts toward an active status. You are no longer only a passive "withstander." Much rather you record the observed and protocol it. This approach proves to be less time consuming than the diary.

The family consists of:

B. Creemers, 34 years old
A. Creemers, 30 years old
S. Creemers, 12 years old
L. Creemers, 6 years old
P. Creemers, 4 years old

In December 2012, we moved to a new apartment. Since then, we have noticed the following abnormalities:

The Haunting Diary

Phenomenon	In the presence of	Frequency	Remark
Bursting light bulbs or coming loose of their sockets	A., B.	Very often	
Getting pelted with a mobile phone in an unnatural trajectory	A.	Once	Damage of the cell phone
Bending of a crucifix	A., B.	Once	
Hearing steps from the 1st floor although nobody is there	A., B., S.	Often	At different times of the day and night

61

The Haunting Diary

Turning of the pictures on the wall	No one	Often	It happens during the night or when nobody is at home.
Untwisting of the bike valves whenever they are in the basement	No one	Reliably, whenever the bikes are in the basement	Merely an old man has access to the basement who is a friend of the family
Things fall out of the shelves in the supermark et	A., B.	Less often	Without a reason, things fall out of the shelves and to the ground behind A. and B.

The Haunting Diary

Vibration of the bed	A., but mainly B.	Very often	Even at B.'s place of work
Washing machine and dryer constantly breaking down	No one	Often	The devices are in the basement; they frequently cause flooding
Spotting of "shady guises"	All family members	Often, right after moving in; currently not	
S.'s TV turns on by itself	No one	Often	At different times of the day, but only when nobody is in the room

The Haunting Diary

Breaking down of electric devices when they are most needed	A., B.	Often	Cell phone, navigation device, water boiler etc.
Turning of the kitchen clock 180 degrees	No one	Once	In the morning, B. and A. realize that the kitchen clock had turned
Decaying of refrigerated groceries long before the date of expiry	No one	Often	Contin-uously noticed by all family members

The Haunting Diary

Altogether this table shows a varied mixture of phenomena, although it is only an extract. I listed the most prominent incidents or the ones noticed for the first time.

It proves to be a big challenge to keep our kids away from these things. My wife and I agreed that it cannot be conducive for their development if they are being confronted with haunting appearances. Obviously, it is impossible to keep everything a secret, but usually they only attach as much value to these incidents as their parents do. For that reason, we ignore every abnormality or denote it as an unimportant coincidence whenever they are present. Fortunately, my wife and I have managed to keep the kids out of this issue for the most part. I hope that this will also be the case in the future. I also believe that it would only be coincidence if they were to notice anything about the haunting and that they are not the main target of the phenomena.

*

Search for answers

There are different hypotheses for haunting. On the one hand, there is the classic one assuming that haunting deals with ghosts walking abroad, in the widest sense of the word. This *spiritualist* assumption explains the multitude of "paranormal" phenomena with the action of a decedent's soul or other spiritual beings. With that in mind, we can use the spiritualist theory to explain haunting appearances in one place, which have been lasting for centuries, as well as individual-related haunting only lasting for a few weeks. Methods like *automated writing* or *channeling* are actively used by spiritualists in order to establish contact with the beyond. In doing so, they utilize a particularly talented individual – a so-called medium who, due to a special susceptibility and sensibility, is capable of putting himself in a trance that enables him to communicate with the ghosts. The required profundity of the trance differs between each medium.

On the other hand, we have the animistic theory that considers a so-called focus person as the main cause for supernatural phenomena. According to this theory, such a person is unconsciously displacing problems to the outside, where these problems are the cause for haunting appearances. In this case, we are talking about an unconscious psycho kinesis which cannot be controlled by the focus person. Even the fact that certain places are repeatedly being haunted should be caused by those who are present, directly observing it. People who have a corresponding predisposition are known to unwillingly cause paranormal phenomena under certain circumstances. An old building that makes a scary and creepy impression and that allows for several anecdotes based on a general superstition would also lead to spontaneous triggering of haunting phenomena in the presence of such a person.

There are further hypotheses which shall not be attached with any value at this point, because the listed ones already describe the essential difference between the distinct viewpoints. According to my opinion, we cannot consider one hypothesis as generally applicable as the spectrum of paranormal appearances only allows for one conclusion: there are cases that can be justified in an animistic sense as well as cases that can be justified in a spiritual sense, or both. I am convinced of the fact that haunting happens over and over again, but it escapes our notice. The term JOTT (just one of those things) perfectly describes these daily, strange incidents that are normally not bestowed with any further consideration.

One thing is for sure: Haunting takes place wherever people are. People observe it and it influences them. The life of a family directly affected changes. These major changes in life impact the haunting in turn. The phenomena change in kind, intensity and frequency. If you change the way you deal with the experienced phenomena, they also change. Ignoring or denying, for example, often leads to an aggravation of the situation, whereas an active contention with the problem can lead to alleviation. That is not a written law, however, and there are numerous exceptions, but this correlation has proven to be true in a multitude of cases. Therefore we can say that communication takes place between human beings and haunting. This awareness is extremely relevant for each and every victim! They have the chance to act upon incidents and are not only victims in this theatre of absurdities and violations against the good judgment call.

Search for answers

Nevertheless, these animistic theories did not really seem to fit my personal experiences. I suspected that I was actuator and recipient at the same time. Independent of my person, there had to be something that was approaching me during these appearances. Regardless, I had the strong impression that I was always contributing in some way. During my search for answers, I read everything related to haunting and occultism that I could get my hands on which resulted in a substantial and respectable store of pertinent literature. By now, I believe to have seen every single haunting documentation in the German or English language that is circulating the internet. Meanwhile, I came across a movie related to this topic which showed the protagonist called Joerg Schreiber. In this documentation, Mr. Schreiber visited two women who said to be afflicted with haunting. They were living together and reported several different phenomena and the anxiety they caused. Mr. Schreiber was trying to find the cause within the spiritual realm by setting up a special but rather unspectacular way of communication with the spirit world. He walked through the apartment and looked around the rooms. Thereby, the two women told him about their experiences. At a point that seemed to be suspicious according

Search for answers

to him, he closed his eyes and entered an "ethereal" level . At this level, Mr. Schreiber was apparently capable of communicating with the unsolicited visitors. He described deceased individuals he clearly saw and started negotiating. The aspiration was to try and guide those restless ghosts to a "different level." I personally interpret this "different level" as the beyond. At the end of the procedure, Mr. Schreiber assured the two women that they would now have their peace, because the said troublemakers were gone. The success showed for itself as the haunting stopped and the two woman were highly satisfied with the performance of the "ghost expeller." Nevertheless, Mr. Schreiber indicated that the unsettled ghosts could find their way back to the apartment due to the structural circumstances given. Principally, I would critically face such an approach, but it was very convincing in a way nonetheless. He seemed very natural and it did not seem to bother him what other people thought of his work. There is a saying in the field of medicine: *The one who can heal is right*. This expresses that the aim is only of minor importance as long as it is reached. Due to the fact that I could not lose anything, I contacted this man myself, via e-mail. I described my own experiences and asked for a personal evaluation of the situation. Several days later, he replied and requested a picture of me in order for him to examine my "aura." I acknowledged this rather confusing request, because I always thought that one could only see an aura – if it even exists – on a living person and not a photograph. However, if you contact somebody who claims to be able to get in touch with ghosts, such a request should not be surprising. Therefore, I sent him the picture and while I was waiting for his reply, I obtained some information about Mr. Joerg Schreiber in the meantime. He had written a book and operated a homepage that he used for explaining his view on supernatural instances. I now knew that he did not only deal with supernatural phenomena on the side as this topic obviously seemed to by occupying a big part of his life. After a few days, I received his assessment of my picture via e-mail. Only on the basis of my picture, Mr. Schreiber seemed to be able of determining that I had extraordinary "medial potential," but was unable to exhaust it. Ghosts of deceased individuals would still recognize this ability and try to catch on with me. Since I was not using my medial potential, those spiritual beings would desperately try to make themselves felt and I only had to listen with both ears to understand them. That is also how he explained the haunting phenomena that have been intriguing me for almost thirty years. The anxiety that kept overcoming me all of the sudden and the continuously reappearing impression that the indoor climate would change, also fit this theory well. I accepted his explanation and started to interpret all haunting appearances as an attempt of different ghosts to get in contact with me. At first, this hypothesis offered a comprehensive explanation in my case, although it did appear somewhat adventurous. But why exactly were the dead so interested in me? What kind of service could I deliver? If Mr. Schreiber's words were to be true, it still would not make any sense to me. Somebody who has experienced haunting appearances before has a hard time discounting something as untrue without having verified it beforehand. For a few years already, I am working part-time as a therapeutic hypnotist and I am therefore accustomed to trance conditions. In addition to that, I was aware of the fact that many mediums would utilize trance in order to exercise their abilities. For that reason, I thought it was obvious to undertake a few attempts in trance. If there was a hidden communication channel, the critical consciousness might prohibit it from functioning right. The thought behind it was to partly avoid the "scrutinizing self" through hypnosis, in order to initially find out whether I could successfully achieve an effect in my surroundings by self-suggestion. For this purpose, I sat down at my desk on a quiet evening and put myself in a low trance by using a relaxation technique. I chose a simple suggestion that left lots of room for interpretation by claiming that there would be a specially obvious and unaccountable change visible in our apartment the following morning. I repeated this suggestion multiple times and finished with a formula that helped my anchor my suggestions:

"The subconscious mind is a superpower and everything that has been said will happen exactly the way it was said, because that is how it is right."

I did not expect anything to happen, but was not surprised to find numerous cabinets in the kitchen with opened doors and drawers the next morning. Moreover, a sheet metal sign and a spice rack had fallen from the wall to the ground. Both objects had to have landed and stayed on the countertop if they simply fell off the hook. Instead, they were

Search for answers

lying in the middle of the room, a location they could not have reached on their own. Of course it was also plausible that this was the result of a "normal" haunting incident and not my suggestion. However, I had the impression as if this was not a random event, and I could often reliably trust my intuition with regard to other cases in the past. The next step would have been comprised of the attempt to contact whatever wanted to communicate with me. Assuming that it would turn out the way it was postulated by Mr. Schreiber, I would have put myself in trance and established contact to something that I was afraid of my whole life. Such a process would have amounted to necromancy. Only the thought of that was more than unpleasant. For that reason, I left it at numerous tries to trigger haunting phenomena with the aid of trance and auto suggestion which I was repeatedly successful with. For instance, I succeeded in precipitating targeted incidents, like the blowing of a specified light bulb (The attempts to achieve PSI-effects under hypnosis were extremely comprehensive and will be discussed in a later book). Now the reader is probably wondering why I did not manage to capture something of that sort on film. I am still stuck for an answer, because all attempts to record something in action, failed. Haunting does not like to be recorded as if it was trying to avoid people from proving its existence. This elusiveness is one of its "legitimacies." It seems likely that the filmmaker is being ridiculed by the simple fact that something happens every time the camera has just been turned off. Almost like a shy predator, haunting eludes from direct observation and avoids walking right into the "trap" of the camera. At first glance, this phenomenon combined with the circumstance that there is an existing interaction between haunting and its victims – as I mentioned before – seems to be a clear hint that we are indeed dealing with an intelligent and decision-making being. At second glance, we can determine that that the world of plants also consists of various examples that react surprisingly fast and situation-related to its surroundings. However, no one will ever attribute plants to intelligence or decision-making capability. Maybe it is quite similar to haunting appearances and the reactions it shows are only a rudimental reflex reaction of a rather non-intelligent complex.

*

Comparable cases

Since extraordinary experiences are part of a person's life and one can righteously assume that most people have already made such experiences, I am obviously always keeping ears and eyes open and have long been sensitized for this topic. Normally, it would rarely be the case that somebody steps up and eagerly talks about how his deceased grandmother visited him or reports about reoccurring poltergeist phenomena in the house. But if one listens carefully, asks specific questions and signalizes that one is openly facing this topic, the affected person will normally gladly catch on. The problem is that the possibility of talking about it openly and factually is rarely given.

The comparison of different haunting cases shows that some phenomena are always reoccurring. It seems as if there is a certain existing base repertory that persists independently of all outer circumstances. The

Comparable cases

following appearances keep showing up in the most different cases:

Stone rain

Sudden stone rains within or outside of closed rooms. The stones seem to materialize in the air. In some cases, the perceived origin of the stones could be determined, because they were wet. One implied that they should be coming from a house located by a creek.

Pelting

Individuals are pelted with objects. Thereby, it can happen that said objects previously formed in the air. It can also happen that these objects are flung from their location toward the targeted person.

Temperature drop

Unexpectedly, the room temperature drops. Some people interpret this phenomenon as the energy source for haunting. According to that idea, the heat of the air delivers the required energy for all different phenomena.

Comparable cases

Knocking, steps and rumbling

Knocking noises, steps and rumbling occur in many haunting cases, especially during the initial phase.

Disappearing and reappearing of objects

Objects cannot be found and reappear all of the sudden. Oftentimes, those objects are very warm right after being rediscovered.

Abnormal reactions of animals

Oftentimes, especially dogs feel something in their bones regarding supernatural phenomena. They show obvious fear and behave untypically.

Appearances

Appearances can take place in all kinds of different ways. Humanly figures, light flashes, or misty fogs and shadows are frequently observed.

Comparable cases

Fire

Sometimes one witnesses unexplainable fires that put themselves out and are locally limited.

Olfactory sensations

Sudden appearing of partially strong scents is a consistent part of haunting.

Voices and noises

Acoustic appearances are frequent. This concerns loud calling, incomprehensible whispering or the imitation of everyday life noises (mimicry noises).

Malfunction of technical equipment

Functional disorder in electrical or mechanical systems is frequent.

Being touched

The feeling of being touched, shoved or touched in any other way by invisible hands is

Comparable cases

often reported by haunting victims.

Unexplainable sentiments

The feeling of being watched, threatened or even influenced is consistently perceived.

A case which encompasses everything needed for a haunting appearance, can be described using the example of *Melchior Joller*. The haunting under which the Suisse lawyer and former member of the National Council was suffering along with his family was substantial and enormous in its phenomena. The author *Fanny Moser* has carefully examined this haunting in her book "*Haunting – A riddle of humanity*" and printed Joller's report of his experiences in Stans. At this point, if I have caught your interest, I would like to recommend to read this book, because it contains highly interesting case descriptions and documents the difficulties of investigating haunting cases in a way I have never seen before.

Comparable cases

As lawyer and member of the National Council, Melchior Joller was a respected man in the Stans community. He was neither superstitious nor did he believe in ghost stories. Yet, he was still haunted in his own house. Windows and doors closed as many times as it took for them to break. Fist-sized stones pelted down on his children, furniture and paintings were knocked over. All this was accompanied by a noisy scenery. For that reason, the haunting could not be maintained a secret for long. Hundreds of people showed up to marvel at these indescribable appearances. Desperately, Melchior Joller tried to somewhat preserve normality. A typical, but insufficient authoritative inspection was arranged. However, it did not help finding answers for the countless incidents. When his family was already entirely insecure and frightened, due to the incidents, he still remained level-headed and looked for a scientific explanation for all these different appearances. Nevertheless, at some point, he also became insecure and started to believe that a natural explanation is hardly

Comparable cases

probable. Although numerous respected citizens of Stans witnessed these supernatural appearances, Joller's reputation was strongly damaged as a result of the haunting. He lost credibility and came in for the wildest fraud theories. The affair turned out to be awkward to such an extent that the Jollers had to leave Stans. In 1862, Joller wrote down his experiences in the book called "Depiction of self-experienced, mystical appearances."

Melchior Joller opened up his report with the following words:

"If I had not experienced haunting myself and if I had not been relentlessly thrown at this raging monster as prey, I would have never believed the stories of others. I was able to convince myself of this wild monster's existence, wide awake and during the day. It hit me so unexpectedly and severe, like hardly any other disaster would have been capable of.
My desire for truth induces me to make an undistorted and public testimony.

Comparable cases

Fueled by the hope that one day, science will be able to solve the riddle of haunting. A riddle that caused the whole family to be destroyed and banished from our beloved home."

Joller wrote this report, although he must have been aware of the fact that it would only damage his reputation even more. At the time of publication, he had already abandoned his house and moved to Zurich with his family. Even in Zurich, the Jollers kept experiencing haunting appearances. Later on, they moved to Rome, where Melchior Joller ceased in 1865. Within his report, he factually and impressively describes how haunting can severely affect the life of a family and how one is helplessly facing the infringement.

Because "*Depiction of self-experienced, mystical appearances*" is already printed unabridged with Moser, I refrain from a further presentation of this writing.

Comparable cases

The poltergeist of Enfield

With "The poltergeist of Enfield" we are talking about a haunting case that beset family Harper in the British town Enfield from August 1977 to September 1978. The divorced Mrs. Harper was living in a house with her four children, where they became victims of an extremely severe haunting. The case is of special importance, because the phenomena were confirmed by a multitude of witnesses and official investigations. Social workers, psychologists, priests, haunting researchers, and other people witnessed approximately 1500 paranormal incidents. In the first instance of the haunting appearances, the Harpers mainly noticed scuffling noises in one of the bedrooms. Shortly after, knocking noises set in and a deep voice insulted all residents of the house in the rudest way imaginable. This voice was successfully recorded on tape and it was vainly attempted to much the voice with a person. The voice itself claimed to be a 72-year-old man from the neighborhood, which could not be further verified. In addition, the family saw self-ignition of various articles of clothing, paper and a matchbox. All the fires went out by themselves and strongly limited in their spread. Silverware and other household appliances bent by themselves. A photographer was hit in the head with a brick. Furniture flew through the air. The focus of the appearances was directed toward 12-year-old daughter Janet who was used for transmitting a deep voice that insulted all those present in an evil way. Several times, Janet was even floating through the air in her room. Moreover, Janet and her sister were thrown out their beds at night which is the reason why they preferred to sleep on the floor. As time went by, the family started to get used to the strange phenomena. Initially, the mother and her four children panicked and were scared for their lives, but the horror gradually gave way for a general perplexity and confusion. In 1979, the haunting came to an abrupt ending. There was not another single phenomenon which only left confused scientists as well as

Comparable cases

witnesses. The poltergeist of Enfield is a typical example for a haunting case which uses a child as the central focal point. In this case, representatives of the animistic theory will immediately see the reason in the girl's imminent puberty and the corresponding mental and emotional conflicts. The parents' divorce and the new surroundings could also be another reason for an externalization of an inner conflict. In spite of the obvious cause, we should not completely ignore a spiritualist approach. Could the emotional condition of the girl have possibly attracted ghosts or something similar? Do these creatures have an affinity for humans in a difficult psychological situation?

The typical ghost castle

Edinburgh Castle is one of the most significant sights in Scotland. The more than 900-year-old walls are said to accommodate numerous ghosts and there are just as many logged reports of extraordinary appearances within the castle. In fact, a headless drummer is said

Comparable cases

to be playing next to a bagpipe-playing ghost. Even ghosts of French prisoners from the Seven Year War and other soldiers from the American War of Independence line up for the total stock of regular ghosts. The story of Edinburgh Castle is full of atrocious incidents, ranging from human harm and torture to death.

Castles seem to be awkwardly dark and threatening at night. The observer does not expect anything good to happen behind the thick doors. That is how sensory mistakes develop.

Comparable cases

Therefore, it can be considered the ideal location for haunting. It is no wonder that, even today, people are still convinced to have seen ghosts in the old ruins. If haunting were a play, such a castle would be the perfect stage. Everybody willingly looking for such a place must already be expecting something strange to happen. This expectation deceives the competence to judge in a way that necessitates one to look at reports of haunting in such old castles highly critical. A strong blow of the wind, an unknown noise and a shade – there is your haunting experience for starters.

*

Haunting or foolishness?

Repeatedly, we see incidents in our daily routine that we cannot explain. Especially if we are under stress, we tend to forget one thing or another and in the end, we are facing the outcome of our own action without being able to remember any of it. In this case, one would not generally think of paranormal phenomena in the first place. The way we perceive things, heavily depends on the individual experiences and the momentary situation in life. On top of that, the way people are raised, along with specific social norms, also play an important role in the interpretation of certain occurrences. Every human being has a unique wealth of experiences and evaluates according to his or her own standards. In every haunting case, however, people start to reach a point where they are incapable of finding a "natural" explanation. Our sense of perception differs between one another. Therefore, the point in time, when we actually perceive a haunting appearance as such, is also different. Sometimes it is never recognized at all and sometimes we start to read something into it which could be explained a different way. A generally applicable indicator is non-existent. Then how do we determine whether or not one is being haunted or simply foolish? When this question arises, there is at least a suspicion at hand and the possibility of a supernatural influence will be contemplated. This altered viewpoint alone, regarding one's daily routine, is reason enough for the recognized phenomena to change. Others can appear in addition, common ones disappear or the overall intensity changes. For that reason, assuming that a person's mental health as well as the ability to judge is given and this person conceives suspicion based on different abnormalities, one will oftentimes notice a corresponding reaction of the haunting – if it really is haunting. This alteration, achieved through a changed perception, is a hint toward real haunting. In order for this statement to be true, we always have to presume an adequate ability to judge of the person affected. Once one accepts the plausibility of haunting, he or she will usually start to view the past abnormalities in a different light. In doing so, it is necessary to reflect prudently, because not every single abnormality can be blamed on haunting.

Psychologically-ill people will experience more difficulties identifying the haunting compared to supposedly healthy ones. Many extraordinary experiences feature an antagonist in pathology. In some of those cases, the boundaries are non-limiting. "Hearing voices" is a good example for illustrating how difficult it can be to differentiate between supernatural phenomena and psychiatric symptoms. People who are suffering from schizophrenic psychosis are known to hear voices in some cases that command them, bother and harass them or catch on in a different kind of way. These voices are actually heard and cannot be mistaken for loud thoughts or anything comparable. On the other side, victims are consistently hearing voices when experiencing haunting cases and even completely healthy people can hear voices that occasionally have notice of circumstances unknown to the listener. Officially, a person is only considered psychologically healthy as long as the patient is not diagnosed otherwise. For that reason, it is plausible that a completely healthy person, who is suffering from haunting, decides to go see a psychiatrist and is then confronted with a diagnose that attests lack of judgment, although the patient is in full command of his or her mental faculties. With that said, I am asking myself the question how many people actually get treated who are not sick, but rather impacted by paranormal phenomena. Personally, I am aware of a case where a woman had reported to her family about unexplainable incidents within the household for several weeks. She claimed to be supernaturally influenced. She had affiliated to an esoteric circle and since then, she went through a change in her personality. Initially, one would assume that this woman is a case for the psychiatrist, because she showed strong aggressions, retreated to her darkened bedroom on a regular basis and was full of fear of an unknown power. Possibly, there was also a mental illness, but the problem was not solely a psychological one. Her husband was clueless when he saw his wife cowering perseveringly for hours on end. He called the community's pastor and depicted his problem. The family was living in a rural area and it was common to utilize pastoral care in the midst of various family problems. After the pastor had listened to the husband's story, he entered the bedroom in which the wife was still cowering on the bed, in complete darkness. When he started talking to her, she immediately showed an impetuous reaction and scuffled with him, whereupon he backtracked to the kitchen. Thereupon, they called a doctor, the police and an ambulance, because they were planning to put the woman in a closed psychiatric clinic. Everybody assembled in the hallway and went upstairs collectively in order to overcome the woman. A large expenditure of force was needed to capture the woman on the bed and dope her with a suppressant injection. She was injected a ten milligram dose of diazepam whereupon she calmed down and stopped cursing and insulting the pastor. Normally, such a dose lasts for several hours. In her case, she had already regained all her strength in a matter of minutes and attempted to defend herself against the transportation to the psychiatric clinic. She literally raged, insulted all those present and prompted them to have intercourse with her. A renewed injection only led to short success again. In the end, they had to shackle her, before taking the woman into the psychiatric clinic. I am unaware of the further course of events. The husband reported about unexplainable phenomena that he had observed since his wife had affiliated to this esoteric circle. For instance, he saw how dishes washed themselves and heard random knocking noises throughout the house. In addition to that, he experienced cold sensitivities and described the frequent malfunctioning of various technical devices. He had simply taken note of all these phenomena in disbelief.

In its entirety, this case seems to be a confused story about delusion, religious influence, esoteric hustle, and helplessness. Hardly anybody would proceed from the assumption that haunting actually took place in this case. But why should we

Haunting or foolishness?

dismiss this possibility immediately, just because she does not necessarily fit the picture? By all means, it is also conceivable that, due to a psychological state of emergency that the whole family entered because of the mother's esoteric interest and hysteric behavior, is also reason for evoking the haunting phenomena. At least two circumstances favor the assumption that there could have possibly been supernatural influences. On the one hand, I am talking about the haunting appearances reported by the father and on the other hand, I am referring to the mother's non-namable reaction to a high dose of a strong suppressant. The latter is pharmaceutically explainable, but still conspicuous within this context nonetheless. One-hundred-fifty years ago, people would have most certainly tried to help this woman with an exorcism, without paying attention to any possible psychological causes. Nowadays, doctors completely ignore para-psychological causes and stubbornly treat according to the advisable methods of the current time. I would like to denote both approaches as narrow and illiberal. On the basis of this example, we can see how easy it can be to explain extraordinary experiences with psychological causes, if the targeted person shows a

Haunting or foolishness?

corresponding background. But even in those cases it pays off to watch and listen closely, because mental exceptional cases are, at least from an animistic perspective, good agars for supernatural appearances.

*

False behavior

Although I am not able to deliver a useful answer to a lot of questions, I do know when to alert people to some behavioral patterns. There are a lot of confused people living on our wonderful planet. Of course, they also have the right and freedom to spread their opinions and recommendations in books, videos and the internet. Formulating a hypothesis is legitimate in any case, even if it is incredibly ungraceful. According to my point of view, it gets problematic if these recommendations are made by people whose only goal is to influence others with their way of looking at things. Esotericism offers a high degree of answers and explanations for various life situations, and especially supernatural experiences. If you should encounter somebody, in your search for help, whose view of life is shaped by a belief in angels, this person will also recommend concerning oneself with angels, because they are naturally responsible for everything that brought up the matter in the first place. Such an approach, however, involves great danger for the user. On the one hand, this person closes one's mind to other views and stands in

False behavior

one's own way of trying to find a solution or realization. On the other hand, one's lifestyle could fall to pieces when one starts to make angels responsible for personal skills and spends a large amount of time dealing with this character. In the worst case scenario, this could lead to occupational phenomena and victims will have the impression as if they were haunted by a demon or angry angel. At that point, committing oneself to a psychiatric clinic will inevitably be the last option. I do not want to blame anybody for his or her belief in angels. However, with all these angels and their ministry on our lives, it is important to not give away control. In the end, we are individually responsible for our fortune and misfortune. Self-perception obviously changes when one is following an esoteric trend. Therefore, a self-appointed witch will interpret an extraordinary perception different than a person who does not deal with esotericism at all.

In case of adverse preconditions, occult techniques like moving glasses around or the Qui-Ja board can lead to an aggravation of the problem or, in case of no existing problem, precipitate such. Such "evocation techniques" can lead to extraordinary experiences that trigger dread.

False behavior

Young adults are especially endangered. Principally I can say there are serious consulting services that offer helpful advice and assist the victim in recognizing the problem. An objective listener and experienced advisor can still your fear to a certain extent and is the first person of contact in many cases.

A checklist for those affected could look somewhat similar to this:

- At first, do not talk about your problem with anybody.

- Do not let yourself get blown away and keep your power of judgment. Not everything is attributable to haunting.

- Seek talks with serious advisors and give up esoteric Hocus Pocus.

- Carefully observe what happens. Is there a focus person?

- Interpret all the phenomena. Can a message be identified?

- Get accustomed to other haunting cases.

False behavior

> That way, you realize that you are not alone with your problem.

- You have to accept that haunting is part of the human's nature.

Only in the rarest cases, humans have actually been hurt. Most haunting cases are very limited time-wise and those affected will most certainly be left alone soon. However, If you should feel like me and you are continuously dealing with haunting, then you will probably start pursuing your own investigations and face up to this topic more intensively than this book does.

*

Haunting and science

Whether it is a toothbrush, hand lotion, deodorant or detergent – advertising knows: we only start believing in the effectiveness of a product once it has been "scientifically" proven. But what does that actually mean? In a nutshell, scientific evidence is provided when a thesis can be proven under laboratory conditions. Considering that, the effect examined has to repeatable on a reliable basis. For example, formulating a thesis which states that water boils at one hundred degrees Celsius will induce people to install gadgetry, which is capable of heating up the water to said temperature, in a laboratory. Afterwards, the course of the experiment will be documented with appropriate measuring instruments. If the experiment was successful and the thesis confirmed, it gets repeated multiple times in order to confirm the result. In the end, one has scientifically proven that water boils at hundred degrees Celsius. Scientific methods are therefore suitable for attesting effects that abide by certain regularities. Unfortunately, paranormal incidents, like haunting, mainly abide by one rule, namely

101

Haunting and science

the rule of elusiveness – volatility. Haunting seems to elude from direct observation. This predominantly happens when the observer believes in haunting and wants to catch sight of it. The hobby-ghost hunter, who sits on watch with his or her camera, has therefore worse chances of actually seeing supernatural appearances than someone who suspects a natural explanation behind the phenomena. This fact is known from hundreds of well-documented haunting cases and allows for the assumption that scientific methods are utterly useless for researching haunting. Not least because of this reason, parapsychology is still contested up to this day. Nevertheless, we did not lack in experiments that carefully examined the science behind haunting cases and other paranormal phenomena. The U.S. American botanist and parapsychologist *Joseph Banks Rhine* (1895 – 1980) undertook comprehensive laboratory experiments with the goal of proving or contradicting extrasensory perception and psycho kinesis. His studies and examinations generated significant results in part and at least psycho kinesis and extrasensory perception could actually be considered as proven in that sense. Unfortunately, these results get ignored for the most part, similar to the results of works by Max

Haunting and science

Dessoir (1867 – 1947), Hans Driesch (1867 –1941), Albert von Schrenck-Notzing (1862 – 1929), Charles Robert Richet (1850 – 1935), William Crookes (1832 – 1919), John Beloff (1920 – 2006), William G. Roll (1926 – 2012), and many other personalities who have rendered outstanding services to the recognition of parapsychology as a science. Therefore, we do have existing scientific methods that are suitable for examining phenomena that seem to actively elude from a closer visual inspection. However, even the best examination is useless if nobody takes note of its results. I could imagine that it is rather complicated for a researching academic to deal with something that is subject of many scary horror movies. One or another shake of the head by the colleagues is probably of a surety. Maybe this is the reason for recognizing something for the rejection, something that surely deserves more attention, as it is part of the human's nature. All the more high we need to rate the commitment and dedication of those who completely address themselves to parapsychological research.

Haunting and science

When you deal with parapsychology, and especially haunting, in Germany, you cannot get around one name. Dr. Dr. Walter von Lucadou is a German physicist and psychologist and has devoted his work to parapsychology. He is the founder and leader of the Parapsychological Clinic of the Scientific Association for the Promotion of Parapsychology in Freiburg. He continuously presents openly and propagates his system theory of haunting in this particular function. It seems to me as if Mr. von Lucadou intends to press every single paranormal activity into his haunting model with all might and main. In doing so, he completely dismisses the possibility of other theories, although they appear to be more plausible in a given case. According to his opinion, every haunting experience is caused by an underlying psychosomatic disorder. In many cases, this specific interpretation may seem to be standing to reason, but tarring all haunting victims with the same brush does not seem to be the right kind of approach. However, the consulting service of the Association for the Promotion of Parapsychology in Freiburg is surely a good first contact point for all victims, for all the reasons described above. In my opinion, this is Lucadous' true merit, because he takes all haunting victims

Haunting and science

seriously and does not deny their experiences. Haunting and science – These two words appear to be opposites at first sight. Science is responsible for advancing knowledge with research. The methods used have to be chosen according to each respective topic. One will never succeed in measuring air pressure with a thermometer. The right method to research haunting may not have been found yet, but that does not free science of its responsibility to keep track of this phenomenon and further explore it. There are plenty of research possibilities, both in the past and today.

Since I am not a scientist, I would like to refer the interested reader to the numerous works on this topic. Unfortunately, some of those works require lots of patience from the science-uninterested reader. I would like to emphasize and warmly recommend the following two writings as they are an easy and exciting read:

Suisse Haunting and Psychokinesis
Theo Locher/Guido Lauper
Publisher: Aurum

Haunting and science

The Poltergeist
William G. Roll
Publisher: Aurum

Both writings consist of many interesting case examples and factually consider the haunting topic.

*

What are ghosts?

Looking at haunting from a spiritualist perspective, we inevitably ask the question with whom or what we are dealing with. Many people will give one clear answer – with ghosts! But what are ghosts? This expression is inconsistently used. The spirit is used for describing various forms of human thinking. The *spiritus sanctus* – the Holy Ghost – is considered the third person of divine Trinity in Christianity. The human soul is occasionally constituted as a spirit/ghost. Public superstition knows ghosts as bodiless, supernatural creatures that possess human attributes. With their appearance or behavior, they remind us of a human being. Ghosts of this kind are known in every culture and they are mostly interpreted as spiritual remainders of a deceased person, who is incapable of finding his or her peace for some reason. Given this statement, we are therefore dealing with the soul of a human being when we are exposed to haunting? But why would a deceased individual wander around the earth and harass other people? Personally, I could hardly imagine what would possibly have to induce me to

What are ghosts?

act on earth as a ghost during my afterlife. It seems like an impractical and pointless waste of time. Possibly, the soul's remaining in our world is not a voluntary act – a punishment for somebody who has burdened oneself with lots of guilt in life. The motivation of a homicide victim could possibly be the unsolved act; or maybe the soul does not know what to do next and is in despair, because it does not understand its condition at all. Nobody can accurately answer this question and we will not know until we also depart this life. Or is it also possible at times that the ghost leaves the body prior to the official death certificate? How does this assumption relate to apallics whose brain functions are reduced to an absolute minimum?

Potentially, the soul is located in the cerebrum and has long left these peoples' bodies. There are many questions and not a single binding and generally applicable response.

What are ghosts?

On the way to the light. People who were on the cusp of the beyond describe near-death experiences somewhat similar to this.

What are ghosts?

Near-death experiences could possibly bring a little light into the darkness, because they immediately seem to deal with the question of life after death. Near-death or maybe even short-death? In fact, these incidents appear with people who already seem to have darkened death's door. A doctor will pull a different line between life and death than a theologian would. A lawyer could have a third opinion regarding this matter. I believe that, in relation to near-death experience of a person, only the personal experience as well as the conviction of it matters. Someone who has already made such an experience will have an answer to this question. The way these people report on their experience and the complete conviction of having been on the cusp of the beyond strongly impress me. Conspicuously, in many cases, the descriptions of the process of "dying" equate to each other in some distinct points.

In 1975, the American psychiatrist and philosopher Raymond A. Moody published a book concerning his collected reports about near-death experiences. He summarizes these experience reports as follows:

110

What are ghosts?

"A human is dying. While his physical affliction nears its peak, he hears how the doctor pronounces him dead. Suddenly, he recognizes an unpleasant noise, a penetrating ringing or buzzing, and at the same time, he feels like rapidly moving through a dark tunnel. Afterwards, he is suddenly situated outside of his body, but still in the same surroundings as before. As if he were an observer, he looks at his own body from a distance. Wrought-up in his feelings, he witnesses the attempts at resuscitation from his strange observation post. After some time has passed, he recovers himself and starts to get evermore accustomed to his strange condition. He discovers that he still possesses a 'body' which, however, differs in consistency and abilities compared to the physical body he has left behind. Soon, new incidents are taking place. Other creatures approach the dying person in order to greet and help him. He catches sight of the spiritual beings of relatives and friends already deceased. In addition, a light and warmth emitting creature appears in front of him – a light being he has never seen before. This creature – without using a word – addresses a question to him which is meant to induce him to rate his life as a whole. It helps him by subjecting him to a panorama of the

What are ghosts?

most important events in his life in a lightning-fast retrospection. At one point, the dying person believes to be approaching some kind of gate or border that obviously symbolizes the separating line between the material and the following life. But he realizes that he has to return to Earth, because the time of his death has not come yet. He strives against this sensation, because his experiences with the life in beyond have captured him so intensely that he does not wish to turn around. He is deeply steeped in emotions of happiness, love and peace. Despite of his inner resistance, and without knowing how, he reunites with his physical body and continues to live. He faces huge difficulties at later attempts trying to tell other people about his experience. For a start, he is incapable of finding any human words that could accurately describe the kind of unearthly incidents he witnessed. When he also notices that he is not treated with respect, but much rather scorn and taunt, he gives up telling other people about it altogether. Nevertheless, the incident leaves behind deep marks in his life; it particularly influences the way each respective person confronts death and understands its relation to life." (Source: Moody, 1989, 27-29 – the original text is also written in cursive)

What are ghosts?

One should try to portray himself into same situation, with the only difference that his way back to life is blocked, although he leaves family behind who needs him. Possibly, one would attempt to escape from this transfer into another world in order to be able to continue carrying out one's duties on Earth. Assuming one actually had this option and one would elude from the beyond, without an earthly body at one's disposal, what would be the next step? Based on this circumstance, one would have to attune to strong confusion and frustration. Maybe there would be many open questions, but no person of contact, which would induce the desperate victim to get in touch with other people or fellow sufferers. Could it be possible that, in relation to haunting, desperate people, without an earthly body, are trying to catch our attention? Question upon questions, and one answer actually immediately suggests itself. We only have to be patient and we will find out one day. In my job, I often have to deal with death. Oftentimes, I come over the feeling of unknowing in the presence of a corpse. This human being, lying to my feet, already knows the answer to all of my questions – simply by the circumstance of having parted from life. However, the human is known for being eager for know-

What are ghosts?

A shadowy observer in the dark. Ghostly appearances within the frame of haunting are related to the phenomena that can trigger paralyzing fear.

114

What are ghosts?

ledge and impatient at times. For that reason, we sometimes occupy ourselves with things that could simply be sat out.

*

Small encyclopedia of the occult

Animistic haunting theory

We assume that haunting appearances originate from the psyche of a so-called focus person. Especially pubescent adolescents are said to be in the focus of these haunting appearances that they trigger unconsciously.

Apportation

In parapsychological terms, apportation describes the unexplainable transportation of certain objects through walls or over a great distance. During apportations, firm structures are cut through or distances are covered, without identifying or understanding a specific mechanism.

Astral body

Compared to our solid body, the astral body is considered a subtle body that every human being possesses. It is known to be immortal and, among other things, responsible for our well-being.

Automatic writing
This phenomenon describes contacting ghosts with the aid of a medium, which is then used for writing down texts. This kind of communication with the spiritual realm is practiced by spiritualists.

Extrasensory perception (ESP)
This topic summarizes the kind of phenomena that concern information transfer outside of any known and established communication paths.

Exorcising
Practices of robbing a ghost, object or person the ability to move are constituted as exorcising by public superstition. The impact is triggered by a ritual, for example the smashing of exorcising cones.

Channeling
The term "channeling" originates from the USA and describes a technique during which a medium considers oneself as a speaking tube to the

"spiritual world." This medium opens so-called channels which the "ghosts" can utilize to communicate with the temporal world.

Demonic obsession
The Catholic Church assumes that demons take advantage of weak spots in the personality structure or mental crisis of a person, in order to seize hold of them. Victims of obsession suffer extreme tortures and quite often die from the implications of the obsession. Supernatural phenomena are noticed in the progress of an obsession.

Doppelganger
For centuries, this has been a known phenomenon in all cultures, describing a person who is witnessed in at least two different places at the same time.

Ectoplasm
The term "ectoplasm" has been adopted from biology. Parapsychologists describe it as an invisible or gauzy substance that is said to leak out of a medium.

Small encyclopedia of the occult

Esotericism
Esotericism is a collective term for different ideologies and meaning of life-explaining models.

Evocation
Evocation can be explained as the appeal or summoning of a ghost or another higher being.

Electronic voice phenomena (EVP)
Ghost voices are recorded on an audiotape or digital recorder. These audiotape voices can only be heard when playing the tape. Oftentimes, EVPs end up being incomprehensible noises that only make sense after the listener has interpreted them.

Exorcism
Exorcism is occurring in every culture and describes the procedure of casting out demons. It follows an exactly stipulated course of action.

Aura
In parapsychology, the term "aura" is explained as an assumed energy flow which surrounds a person who is, among other things, responsible for

extrasensory perception or psycho kinesis.

Ghosts

In general, ghosts can be described as creatures that do not possess a material body. Frequently, one assumes that a ghost is the spirit of a deceased person. There is no exact definition of the term.

Ghost photography

Ghost pictures can emerge randomly or on purpose. In the process, something is depicted on the photo that was not visible to the photographer at the time of taking the picture. This can concern a person, animal or object. Oftentimes, only obscure figures are recognizable. Ghost pictures have often been unmasked as forgery in the aftermath.

Ghost visionaries

Ghost visionary is the folksy label for a person who is capable of seeing the ghosts of those deceased or other spiritual beings, without any special preparation.

Small encyclopedia of the occult

Shifting glass
Similar to a Qui-Ja board, one uses numbers and digits, on a flat surface, in order to receive messages from the beyond with the help of shifting glass. The people involved in such a session put one finger on the glass which is then supposed to move.

Divination
The knowledge of concealed things, facts and circumstances can be described as divination.

Kirlian photography
The purpose of Kirlian photography is to make the aura of a person or other being visible by means of photographic methods.

Medium
A person who is capable of establishing contact to the world of ghosts can be described as a medium. Mediums put themselves in a trance and become a speaking tube for ghosts and other supernatural creatures in this condition. There are also mediums that are in a position to achieve this condition in a waking state.

Small encyclopedia of the occult

Mimicry noises
These are noises imitating certain processes (imitation noises). In parapsychology, these kinds of noises appear in haunting, when one can hear noises of the daily life without a designated reason. For example, the noise of rattling dishes, although no one in the household is busy doing the dishes.

Out of body experience
An out of body experience, also known as astral journeying, describes the condition of a person whose so-called astral body has left the physical body, and moves around independently.

Precognition
Precognition can be described as the foreseeing of future events in a supernatural way.

PSI
PSI is a letter in the Greek alphabet. Parapsychologists use PSI to denote presumed and unknown powers of the human.

Small encyclopedia of the occult

Psycho kinesis
Psycho kinesis, or telekinesis, is known as the process under which matter is moved, simply by the conscious thoughts or subconscious mind of a person.

Qui-Ja board
This board, consisting of numbers and digits, originates from the USA and is a tool for facilitating communication with "ghosts" or other supernatural creatures. The name is composed of the French word qui = yes and the German word ja. The messages are displayed on the board, by means of a planchette.

Recurrent spontaneous psycho kinesis (RSPK)
The user of this expression for haunting appearances manifests his theory for this topic by his choice of words. RSPK describes supernatural appearances whose cause is to be found in the psyche of a person.

Séance
During a séance, a so-called medium establishes contact to one or multiple ghosts. In the process,

the medium typically enters a trance state.

Spiritualistic haunting theory
Advocates of this theory think ghosts of deceased individuals are the reason for haunting appearances. Spirits of the deceased are said to wander around the Earth, because they have to convey a message or did not have enough time to finish a certain job during their lifetimes.

Telepathy
Telepathy can be described as an extrasensory information transfer.

Xenoglossia
This phenomenon can be described as the ability to speak foreign languages without having learned them before.

*

Hints for the internet research

The internet has a wealth of information concerning haunting. Some known and some lesser-known haunting cases can be found on various pages in the form of reports. For the interested reader, I would like to suggest the following catchwords when searching the internet:

<u>Haunting in Rosenheim</u>

In 1967, strange things happened in the attorney's office in Rosenheim. Among other things, paintings started to turn on the wall, furniture moved on its own, electronic devices reacted abnormally and pops were heard. The case is interesting in this respect, because it has been meticulously examined by all kinds of specialists and representatives of parapsychology. The result was unambiguous: they could not explain the phenomena.

Hints for the internet research

Haunting in Talpa

Eleonora Zugun, from the Romanic Talpa, is the center of attention in this specific haunting case. This case reports about numerous impressive phenomena. It was examined by the parapsychologist Zoe Wassilko von Serecki.

The prophetess from Prevorst

From 1801 until 1829, Friederike Hauffe came to be known as *the prophetess from Prevorst*. A few years prior to her early death, she is believed to have shown symptoms of "demonic obsession." Haunting appearances and extrasensory perception are said to have occurred. Senior civil physician Justinus Kerner has examined the case.

The haunting case in Neuwied-Oberbieber

In 1991, Prof. Dr. Ernst Senkowski examined a haunting case in Neuwied which is said to have frightened a family with its destructive and threatening phenomena.

Hints for the internet research

<u>The faces from Belmez</u>

Belmez is a village in Andalusia. Since 1971, Maria Gomez' home is afflicted with strange appearances. Faces depict on the floor, the walls, and the ceilings of the house. In 2004, at the age of eighty-five, Maria Gomez died, but the haunting continues until this day. However, all the investigations of the ghostly pictures have not delivered a concrete statement.

The most famous picture from Belmez. Up to this day, thousands have appeared in Maria Gomez' home. Even after her death in 2004.

Personal remarks

Whatever you think about this topic. Disregarding the multitude of currently existing "Ghost Hunter Shows" or the "coolness" of these paranormal phenomena nowadays, there will always be people who experience things that cannot be pigeonholed. In general, haunting and paranormal incidents have occurred long before the pertinent movies and books and they will keep existing, even long after this topic is not considered for the public benefit anymore. The people who experience these things in their private surroundings suffer from fear and have to deal with it on their own. The situation of the haunting victims could be dramatically improved if we would start listening more carefully and go without the despicable wave of the hand. Not everyone who hears bodiless voices is mentally disturbed, and not everyone whose bed suddenly starts dancing around at night has a perception disorder. By publishing this book, I got to meet lots

Personal remarks

of people who struggle with similar or equal problems. On top of that, I have come about some personal insights that I would have never acquired without the exchange with other people.

At this point, I would like to thank *Kai Muegge* for widening my horizon and showing me a different perspective on the world of extraordinary appearances.

With pleasure, I would also like to shine my gratitude on another person, who is still on hand with help and advice for me up to this day, and has a nearly inexhaustible knowledge in the area of macro-psycho kinesis at his command. For protective reasons of the personality, I forego mentioning his name at this point, because it concerns a high official whose reputation could be damaged as a result of the general rejection regarding this topic. Even if I am convinced of the fact that the human being will never be able to explain these processes right down to the last detail, I am still sure to have further advanced toward the answer.

Personal remarks

Dear reader,

Just like me, I hope that you will be able to get one step closer to your answers and that you will never lose interest in this topic.

*

Personal remarks